Save
The Bears

by Jeri Lee C.Ht.

Copyright Jerilee.com

2022

All rights Reserved

ISBN: 9798356081224

Thank you for purchasing
Save the BEARS coloring book

Author Jeri Lee C.Ht.

The wildlife on our planet needs Protection from the humans that co-occupy it with them. Humans are the problem and also the solution to the problem. We must learn to respect, appreciate and share the vastness and beauty of the natural world we share. Bears are a tiny part of this task but an essential part of our global puzzle.

This coloring book is designed especially for adults and teens. It comprises artistic quality coloring pages for enthusiastic participants with creative minds and happy pencils. With a few flowers and butterflies added for a pinch of color, it should be a delight for any adult or teen that loves beauty in their entertainment. It belongs to a series of coloring books primarily focused on saving our planet. Yor can be creative and add the sun with a few clouds for shades in your backgrounds of blue and gold. You now have a project suitable for framing.

With respect for our planet and the disrespect of how its population has treated it either knowingly or unconsciously, I believe we all share the guilt of its destruction and the responsibility of its rescue. I share with you the echoing voices of two of its most recent authorities on the subject and pledge to do my part in helping the planet help itself.

Albert Einstein said: The world will not be destroyed by those who do evil, but by those who watch them without doing anything. Everything that exists in your life, does so because of two things: something you did or something you didn't do. Failure is success in progress.

Stephen Hawking said: Remember to look up at the stars and not down at your feet. Try to make sense of what you see and hold on to that childlike wonder about what makes the universe exist. It is very important for young people to keep their sense of wonder and keep asking why.

We are only the temporary custodians of the particles of which we are made. They will go on to lead a future existence in the enormous universe that made them.

With this series of books Save the Planet, I hope you share these values with me. I was born in 1939 and have watched the planet get small enough to fit into your living room while losing the true meaning of nature. So I am requesting your help in rectifying the damage.

This Book
Belongs To

Your Name

LET THERE BE PEACE ON EARTH AND LET IT BEGIN WITH ME

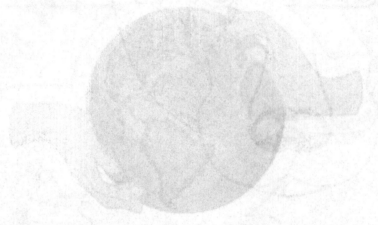

OUR FUTURE
IS IN
OUR HANDS

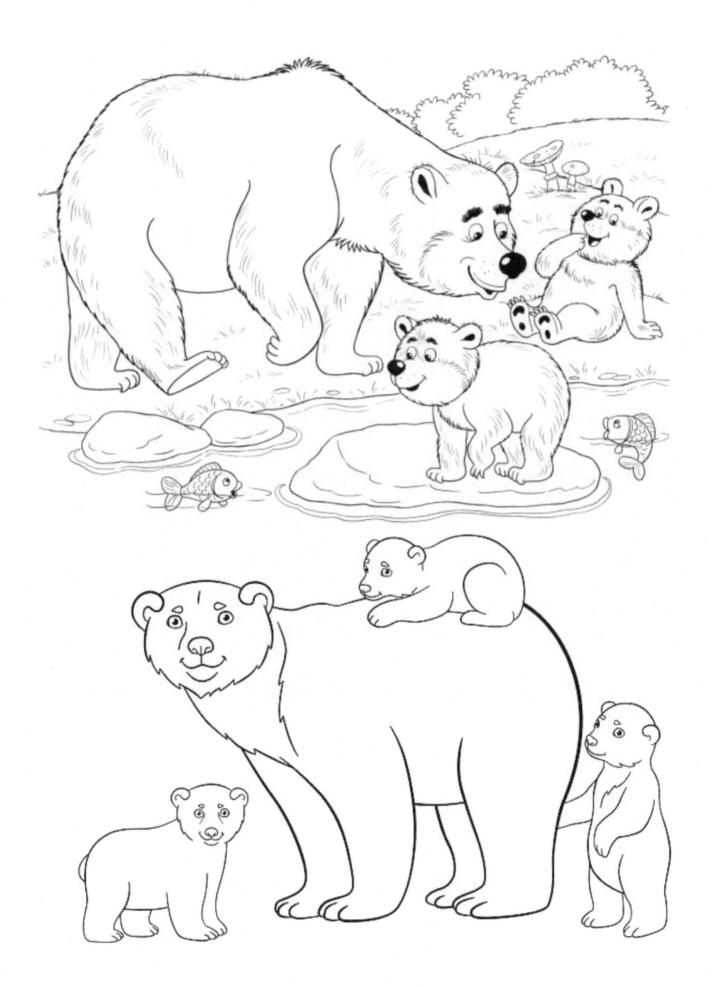

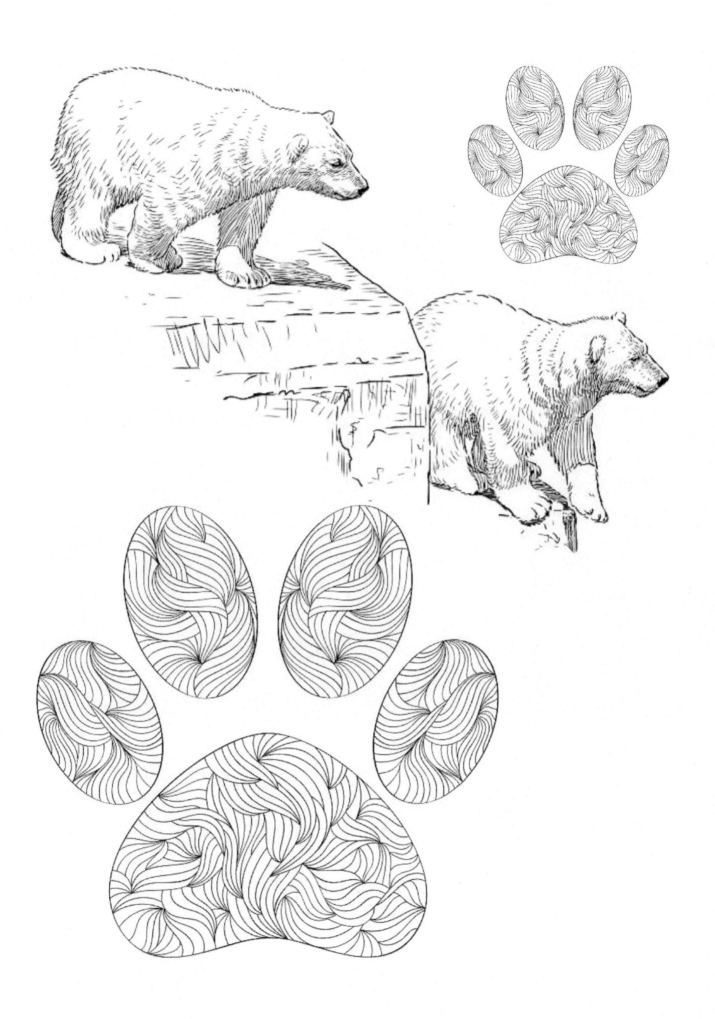

LET THERE BE PEACE ON EARTH AND LET IT BEGIN WITH ME

SAVE THE
KOALA
DAY
SEPTEMBER 24

SAVE THE WILDLIFE
OF AFRICA

LET THERE BE PEACE ON EARTH

AND LET IT BEGIN WITH ME

SAVE THE PLANET

SAVE OURSELVES

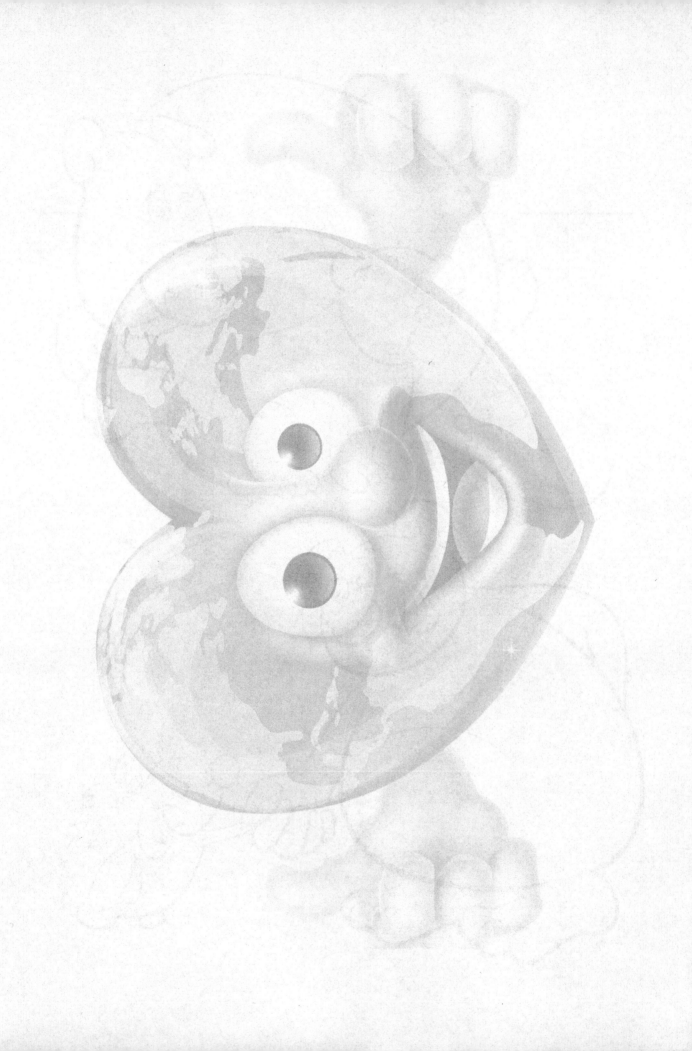

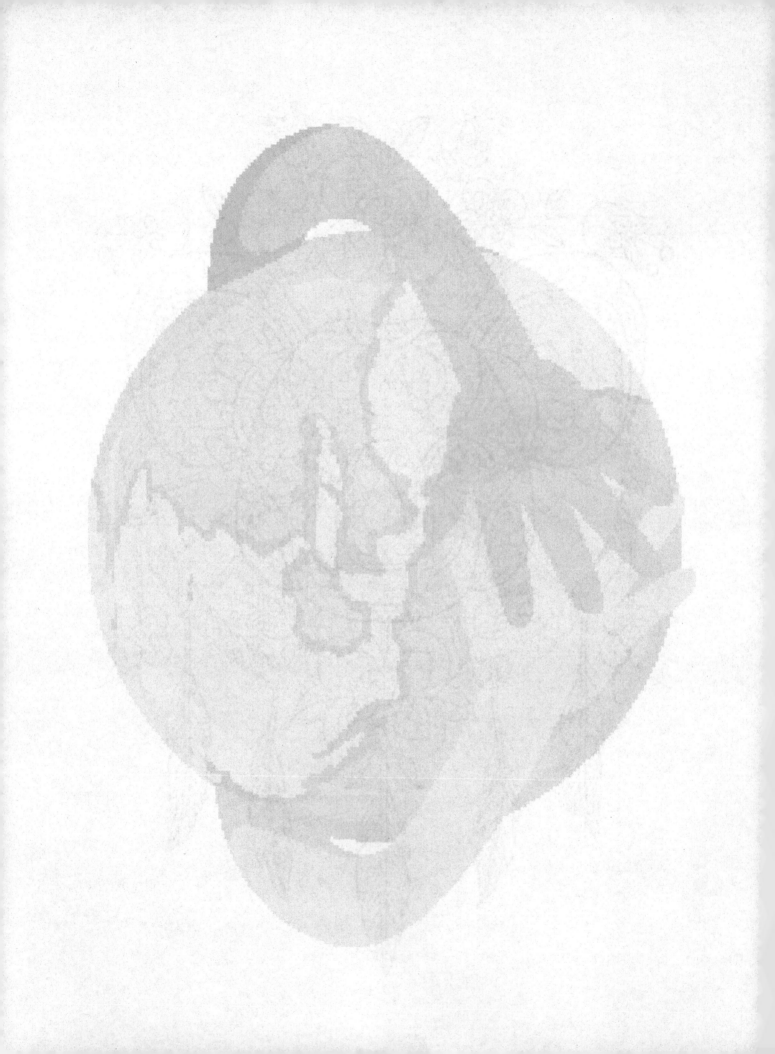

WORLD TURTLE DAY

MAY 23

SAVE OUR PLANET

African Elephant

Asian Elephant

You Might Enjoy

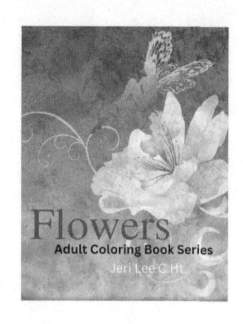

Other Coloring Books

Save the Planet Series
Family Pets Series
Match the Colors Series
Fantasy Series
Flowers & Birds Series
Adult Coloring Book Series

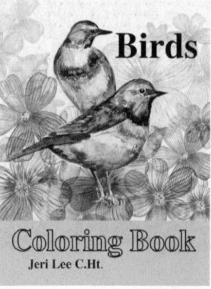

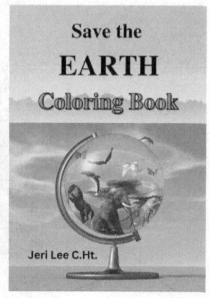

Author
and
Artist
Jeri LeeC.Ht.

Early education is fundamental for the children in our life. The ABCs and 1-2-3s we teach them are the building blocks of their future. We first give them love and care. Then we teach them to walk and talk and right from wrong. Next is their formal education and how to socialize in their environment. It is here that my books can assist. As a mother, grandmother, and great-grandmother, I know that all kids relate to animals, and the first ones they meet are their household pets. Then as they venture out, they meet Farm animals and learn new words like duck, pig, horses, and cows, and they soon discover the habits, sounds, and colors of their new friends. Then a visit to the Zoo introduces them to the world of Nature, and it is essential to teach them to respect without touching our natural environment.

I grew up on a farm and have lived on one most of my life, so it's a subject that comes easy. My coloring books are designed to teach kids to respect the world they live in.

They are published in collectible series with different coloring pages for different ages and interests.

If you like this book, please follow my other series, and if you would give me a good review as an author, I would greatly appreciate it.

UNIVERSAL

PEACE

Made in the USA
Columbia, SC
11 December 2024

49054210R00059